W9-BKC-479

Steven Spielberg

Creator of E.T.

by Tom Collins

DILLON PRESS, INC. MINNEAPOLIS, MINNESOTA

Library of Congress Cataloging in Publication Data

Collins, Tom, 1946-
    Steven Spielberg, creator of E.T.

    (Taking part)
    SUMMARY: A biography of the filmmaker responsible for such popular films as "Jaws,"
"Raiders of the Lost Ark," and "E.T."
1. Spielberg, Steven, 1947-   — Juvenile literature.
2. Moving-picture producers and directors—United States—
Biography   — Juvenile literature.
[1. Spielberg, Steven, 1947-   2. Motion picture producers and directors]
    I. Title.   II. Title: Steven Spielberg, creator of E.T.
PN1998.A3S682   1983   791.43'0233'0924 [B] [92]   83-21068

ISBN 0-87518-249-6

© 1983 by Dillon Press, Inc. All rights reserved

Dillon Press, Inc., 500 South Third Street
Minneapolis, Minnesota 55415

Printed in the United States of America

7   8   9   10   92   91   90

Contents

Summary 5
1 A Little Boy with a
  Big Imagination 7
2 Making Movies of Everything 16
3 "Moviemaking Is Hard Work" 24
4 The Star Wars Connection 38
5 Dreams and Nightmares 45
6 "Movies Are My Life" 56

**This Book Is Dedicated To
Jimmy
For The Best Reason In The World**

Acknowledgments
A special thanks to Steven Spielberg and the staff
of Amblin Entertainment for their encouragement,
support, and assistance in the creation of this book.

STEVEN SPIELBERG

Master filmmaker Steven Spielberg, Hollywood's most successful producer and director, began his movie career as a child. At age 12 he was making home movies of toy train crashes, and four years later he made his first feature-length film. While on summer vacation from high school, Steven joined a group of tourists on a Universal Studios tour. Soon, though, he left the tour group to wander around the studio by himself. Young Steven made friends among the studio workers and was able to return each day to watch the film crews in action. Before he left, he knew that he wanted to devote his life to filmmaking.

From the time he directed his first TV movie for Universal Pictures at age 21, Steven made his mark in the movie world. The films that followed established him as one of the most original and popular filmmakers in movie history. *Jaws, Close Encounters of the Third Kind, Raiders of the Lost Ark, E.T., The Color Purple*, and *Back to the Future* have been seen and enjoyed by many millions of moviegoers.

Today, says Steven Spielberg, "Movies are my life." The youngest director ever hired by a major film studio is now helping other young filmmakers get their chance to direct for the screen. And he, himself, is learning that "there's more to life than movies."

From the Motion picture *E.T.* Courtesy of UNIVERSAL PICTURES.

1. A Little Boy with a Big Imagination

Deep in a mysterious forest overlooking a big valley, a strange-looking spaceship has landed at night. In the darkness a creature from the spaceship breathes heavily as it stumbles over the rough ground.

We sit in the theater audience, watching in silent wonder. Looking at the movie screen, we do not see the creature. Instead, we see and hear what is going on as if we were there in its place.

The tall shadows of men loom among the trees as powerful searchlights pierce the night. We hear their voices but do not see their faces. They are searching the forest for the strange spaceship.

When the men move away, the creature comes to the edge of the forest. As it rises up to look out, we see the valley far below, sparkling with the lights of thousands of houses. Though we do not know for sure, we sense that the being from space will approach the human beings in one of these homes.

This scene is the beginning of *E.T.*, the most successful movie ever shown in America and perhaps the world. Many millions of people, both young and old, have enjoyed the story of the friendship between E.T., the creature from space, and Elliot, a young California boy.

Steven Spielberg—the director of the now famous movie—is the creator of E.T. A master filmmaker, this talented young man has a love for moviemaking that started when he was a little boy with a big imagination.

Steven was born in Cincinnati, Ohio, on December 18, 1947. Soon afterward, Arnold Spielberg, his father, bought a movie camera and began taking pictures of his baby son. Steven knew immediately what to do. He stood up and walked straight for the camera.

Steven's father was a computer specialist. In those days computers were new, and it was exciting to think about what they might be able to do. Arnold Spielberg thought these new machines could help explore the moon and guide rockets into space. He liked to read science fiction stories about exciting space adventures.

One night when Steven was six years old, his father woke him up at two o'clock in the morning so they could go outside and watch a meteor shower together. After watching the "shooting stars" streak across the night sky, Steven decided the sky and stars were worth looking at more carefully.

His mother, Leah, was a concert pianist who used to perform with seven other women. From

(Above) *Guided by his mother Leah, a talented pianist, one-year-old Steven takes his turn at the family piano. (Left) Steven smiling at three years of age.*

her, Steven learned to like music of all kinds. Later, he would use his knowledge of music to make it an important part of his movies.

While Steven was growing up, his family moved three times. When he was 4, the Spielbergs moved to Haddenfield, New Jersey, and five years later they went to Phoenix, Arizona. When he was 16, they went to San Jose, California.

Because his family moved so much, Steven had to get used to many new people and places. The only things that stayed the same were his family and the world he created in his own mind. And Steven made the most of his lively imagination.

When he was seven years old, Steven saw a movie about creatures from Mars attacking the earth. The chief invader looked like a head that was sitting all by itself inside a goldfish bowl. The creature had long arms that looked like octopus tentacles.

Afterwards, Steven hurried home to get a plastic model he had built from a kit. It showed the bones in a human head, and was sitting peacefully in his bedroom. First he put an Air Force cap on top of it. Then he added red lights to make it look spooky. When he was done, he hid his monster in a long, walk-in closet and went to find his three sisters—Ann, Sue, and Nancy.

Steven blindfolded each of them and led them inside the closet. When they took the blindfolds off and saw the terrible thing he had created, they began to scream. They screamed even louder when they found out he had locked the door and they were stuck inside where they could not escape.

He also liked to make up scary stories at bedtime and tell them to his sisters. They would get so excited that they would hide under the blankets. The more they squirmed, the more scary his story would become.

(From left to right) *Steven's sister Ann, Arnold Spielberg, four-year-old Steven, and his mother Leah pose for a family picture.*

Steven found other kinds of mischief to get into, too. "His badness was so original, there weren't even any books to tell you what to do," Leah says. For example, one time he covered the neighbors' windows with peanut butter.

Steven had several parakeets for pets, but instead of keeping the birds in a cage, he let them fly loose. When his mother opened the door of his bedroom, "There would be birds flying around and birdseed all over the floor," Leah remembers. "I'd just reach in to get the dirty clothes."

Each time his family moved, Steven kept having to make new friends. That was not easy for him. He was not good at sports and was usually the last person picked for a baseball team. For a while, he was even called "the retard" because the other kids thought he was different.

In junior high school, Steven was "the weird, skinny kid with acne," he says. And when everyone in class had to cut up a frog, he had to run outside to be sick.

Since Steven wasn't good at sports or meeting people, making movies was a big help. He found he could use them to communicate with people and gain a little bit of popularity. They also gave him something to do after school when all of his friends were playing basketball or baseball, or going out with girls.

"Movies took the place of crayons and charcoal," he says, "and I was able to represent my life at 24 frames a second." That is how fast film moves through a camera. "When I didn't want to face the real world, I just stuck a camera up to my face. It worked."

2. *Making Movies of Everything*

Actually, Steven began making his own movies one hot August night when he found his father's movie camera in the garage. He pointed it into the air and pushed the button.

His first movies were simple ones. Once he had his mother boil a cherry dessert in a pressure cooker until it exploded because Steven wanted to film the mess it made when the walls and floor were all covered with sticky red goo.

Another film served a more practical purpose. When one of the "jocks" in school kept picking on him, Steven invited him to act in a home movie called *Battle Squad*. After that, the bully was more friendly.

To make one of his most exciting early movies, Steven carefully set up two electric trains so that they would run into each other. Then he got his father's camera and filmed the train wreck. He was only 12 years old, but he knew what audiences would like.

Since Steven was so interested in movies, even going camping with him was an unusual experience for his family. For when he was around, everyone became a movie star. Steven made movies of everything. His mother could not open a can of beans for dinner until he got his camera loaded with film.

When Steven got his first movie camera, he joined a Boy Scout photography program. The movie he made for the scouts was only three minutes long, but it told a complete story. One of his friends dressed up in a cowboy outfit and robbed a stagecoach. The picture ended with the outlaw counting his stolen money.

This movie won Steven his first filmmaking award—a Boy Scout merit badge. It also helped him to become, at the age of 13, one of the youngest Eagle Scouts ever.

Before long Steven was spending hours writing movie scripts, and more hours drawing pictures of each shot he would need to film all those movies. Piles of paper began to fill up his room.

Steven's filmmaking really became serious when he went to Arcadia High School in Phoenix. There he discovered the school's theater arts program for people who liked to perform on stage. Suddenly he was not an outsider anymore, for he discovered there were young people interested in the same things he cared about. "That's when I realized there were options besides being a jock or a wimp," he says.

When Steven was sixteen years old, he made his first science fiction movie. It was called *Firelight*, and lasted two and a half hours. Arnold

Spielberg paid the expenses of making the film, which cost $500. Five days a week Steven went to school, and on weekends he worked on the movie.

He did everything himself. He thought up the idea, wrote the script, did his own photography, found the actors and told them what to do, and then edited the film to put it together in its final form.

The movie began with a group of scientists who were searching for the cause of

Steven filming Firelight, *his first feature-length movie.*

mysterious lights in the sky. The lights turned out to be flying saucers, but not friendly ones. The beings inside attacked the scientists, stole an entire city away from the Earth, and then, amazingly, moved it to another planet.

"It was a silly story, but it was fun," Steven says now. He thinks "it was awful," but since the film is lost, no one can judge whether or not he is right about that.

At least it was shown in a real movie theater. Steven talked the manager of the Phoenix Little Theater into giving the film one showing. It not only broke even, but it made a $100 profit.

The next day Steven turned 16, and his family moved to San Jose, California. He went to Los Gatos and Saratoga high schools and kept right on making movies. One of these, called *Slipstream*, was made shortly after Steven finished high school. It was about a bicycle race and starred Tony Bill.

After he moved to California, Steven got to see the inside of a Hollywood film studio for the first time. During one summer vacation, he joined a group on a guided tour of Universal Studios. He waited for a chance to hide, and then let the bus go on without him so that he could wander around on his own.

Soon Steven had made friends with the workers. Each day, he dressed up in a suit and tie and carried a briefcase under his arm. Looking like an important studio worker, he walked right past the guard!

Once inside, he watched the filming of movies and television shows. He even found an empty desk he could use for an office and managed to get the telephone operator to list his name with the switchboard so that he could receive phone calls. Finally, the summer was over. But before he left, Steven told his new friends, "I want to write and direct motion pictures."

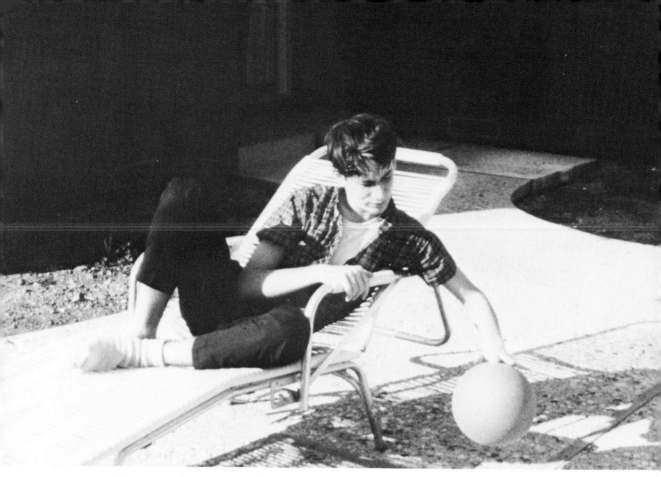

Soon after moving to California, Steven relaxes on the patio.

When Steven finished high school, he wanted to study moviemaking in college. For film students, the best schools in California were U.C.L.A. and U.S.C. Since Steven did not have grades that were good enough to enter these schools, he went to California State College in

Long Beach. Instead of studying, he spent most of his time making more movies and trying to get studio bosses interested in giving him a job.

When that did not work, he decided to prove how good he was. Steven wanted everyone to know that he could move a camera well, deal with lighting and actors, and do all the things a director has to do. Another student, Dennis Hoffman, had made some money from an optical company. He agreed to give Steven $10,000 to help cover the costs of making a movie.

The film took a whole year to finish and lasted only 24 minutes, but it was Steven's best movie so far. Called *Amblin'*, it told a simple story about two young people wandering around together. Some studio bosses at Universal saw it and were so impressed that they gave Steven a long-term contract six weeks before his twenty-first birthday. He was the youngest director ever to get such an offer.

3. *"Moviemaking is Hard Work"*

Steven's first job for Universal was to direct a television movie called *Night Gallery*. In the story Steven directed, Joan Crawford played a rich blind woman who finds an unusual way to regain her sight. After this job, Steven did not work for a year, and then all he did was direct a few programs for different TV shows.

At last Steven had an idea that turned into his first real movie for Universal—a movie that was shown in theaters all across the country. One day when he was looking through an old trunk, he came across some newspaper clippings he had saved. The clippings told about a woman in Texas who had hijacked a police patrol car—with

From the Motion picture *Night Gallery*. Courtesy of UNIVERSAL PICTURES.

Steven Spielberg directs Joan Crawford in Night Gallery.

From the Motion picture *The Sugarland Express*. Courtesy of UNIVERSAL PICTURES.

As smoke rises from the car (rear), *Steven sets up a scene from* The Sugarland Express.

the police officer still in it—to rescue her child from a foster home. He gave the clippings to some old friends and asked them to write a screenplay for a film about that story.

The result was *The Sugarland Express*, starring Goldie Hawn, and it was a success. People liked it, and it made money. The next time Steven Spielberg had an idea for a movie, people in the studio listened to him and made even more money. That film was *Jaws*.

Steven found a copy of the book *Jaws* in someone's office and took it home to read. Then he called the studio bosses and told them the story. They found it easy to imagine a beach resort going crazy because there was a shark in the water eating people.

In fact, the movie does not show the shark attacks in detail because it is so easy for people to imagine them. The most shocking things in *Jaws* happen in people's minds, not on the screen. For example, people get terrified every time they see the sky and water, even when nothing is happening. What they do see makes them expect something to happen at any second.

Steven's special effects were so real that *Jaws* was a hit at the box office. And the film that featured a shark made of rubber won four Academy Awards.

In *Jaws*, much of the time the screen is filled with water, and people are scared by what they

With his hand raised, Steven prepares to take a close-up shot of the shark in Jaws.

From the Motion picture *Jaws*. Courtesy of UNIVERSAL PICTURES.

To make the special effects for Jaws, *Steven often had to direct from a water's-eye view.*

imagine underneath the sea. In *Close Encounters of the Third Kind,* Steven's next success, the sky fills the screen in much the same way. This time, moviegoers keep looking at it and wondering what mysteries it hides, just the way people in the story do.

In some ways, the people in the story are a lot like the people in the audience. "This is the way I grew up," Steven told one of the actresses in the film. "You're living my life."

Watching Steven's movies always makes people feel the story is about ordinary heroes, "real people" just like them. In his films the performers on the screen are behaving the way that the people in the audience would act—or the way they would like to act—if that adventure happened to them. When the actors find themselves in the middle of strange events, the audience goes right along and has the same adventures they do. As Steven says, "All the movies I've made are really about people first."

Close Encounters of the Third Kind is about several ordinary people in the Midwest whose lives are changed when they start seeing flying saucers (close encounters, or meetings, of the first kind). Before long the beings in the flying saucers leave proof behind that they are real (close encounters of the second kind). While the confused humans are trying to understand what is going on, scientists from around the world gather for the landing of one of these alien spaceships (a close encounter of the third kind).

The story centers on a man who repairs telephone lines and a widow whose son has been kidnapped by the aliens. These two humans meet and later sneak into the secret base at Devil's Tower in Wyoming in time to see the landing of the spaceship.

The end of the movie is very beautiful and fills people with a sense of wonder and amazement. The scientists use music and colored lights to talk to the beings on the ship. At last the spaceship lands, and for the first time, people from earth meet travelers from another world. Then some lucky and brave people fly away on the ship to have adventures we can only dream about.

"When I was making this movie, I had dreams that were very strange," Steven says. "I had dreams of being pursued, and being watched, and dreams of things outside my window that were trying to get me to come outdoors. Which I refused to do. I had many of those dreams beckoning to me to leave the house and stand in the backyard. And why was I so frightened about standing out in the backyard when I was asked to go out and look at the sky?"

Steven's imagination about things he could not see or know was quite large even when he was small. When he was a child in New Jersey, there was a crack in the wall that he would notice as he tried to fall asleep. It showed up clearly in the light that came in from the hallway outside his bedroom door. Steven used to imagine that he saw strange creatures living inside the crack. And it seemed to him that they were peeking out and whispering to him to come inside and play with them. In young Steven's imagination, these tiny creatures were real, indeed.

Steven often wonders about the things he cannot see or know.

Right there, in the wall of his ordinary house in an ordinary New Jersey town, was an unknown world that called to him. Today he is still fascinated by the things he thinks might exist but which he cannot see. "There's no proof that flying saucers exist, or that ghosts exist," he says. "But it's always nice to imagine what you think could be there."

"I believe in life in the universe off of this planet," Steven says. But he has never seen a flying saucer. And even though his heart tells him to believe, his head tells him to wait until he has a close encounter of his own. So far, those strange dreams are as close to UFOs as he has ever come. When the movie was finished, the dreams stopped. After that, he could just go outside and look at the stars without worrying that something was calling to him.

Movies, though, have been calling Steven for a long time. He calls movies "my sin," and adds, "I find the people who drink excessively, or take a lot of drugs, aren't really happy with their lives and with what they're doing. But I've been very happy making films, and that is all the stimulation I've needed." Steven rarely drinks, and has no ashtrays in his office.

When he's working on a new picture, Steven creates a family and builds deep friendships. "I kind of shut down my personal life and put everything into my movie world," he says. "It's like having an affair with my film while I'm making it."

But Steven admits that he's often the first one to lose his temper or get pushy as the project takes hold of him. Before long, he says, he becomes a "two-star general." During this period, he becomes moody, stops eating regular meals, loses weight, and doesn't get enough sleep. And when he talks, his sentences start to break up into confused pieces.

"When I work with somebody," Steven explains, "I try to bring the best out of them. Because I'm always trying to bring the best out of my myself with every movie I make. So I get very demanding....Moviemaking is hard work." And the person who works the hardest is Steven Spielberg.

From the Motion picture *E.T.* Courtesy of UNIVERSAL PICTURES.

When Steven makes a movie, he becomes a moody "two-star general." As a director, he must take charge of all parts of filmmaking—the actors, the camera operators, the light and sound technicians, the costume and set designers, and everyone else working on a film. Getting those talented people to work together is a big responsibility.

When the filming stops, Steven relaxes just a little, for his work is far from over. All the pieces of the movie must be put together through editing, and the music for the sound track must be added so that the film and sound blend well. Only then is his director's work finished. At last the movie is ready to be made into the film copies that will be sent to movie theaters around the world.

4. *The Star Wars Connection*

While Steven was a student at Long Beach, George Lucas was a student at the University of Southern California a few miles away. He, too, was making movies and trying to become a director. A few years later, his *Star Wars* movies made him world famous. George and Steven became good friends.

The day before *Star Wars* opened in theaters across America, the two friends were in Hawaii for a vacation to get away from all the excitement. To relax, they built a giant sand castle on the beach and hoped it would bring good luck to the new movie. Steven told George that he wanted to do a kind of James Bond adventure for his next movie. George said he had an idea that was "better than Bond," and he told his friend everything he could think of about it.

After writing the story and guiding the screenplay, George agreed to leave the movie for Steven to make, and trusted Steven's imagination. A year later, when he saw the movie for the first

George Lucas (left, front), *Steven Spielberg* (right, front), *and cast members from George and Steven's new movie,* Raiders of the Lost Ark.

© Lucasfilm Ltd. (LFL) 1981. All rights reserved. COURTESY OF LUCASFILM LTD.

time, he was delighted. "That's how I imagined this movie to be," he said. "Thanks."

The film, *Raiders of the Lost Ark*, is a different kind of movie than *Jaws* and *Close Encounters*. It is an adventure story in which the hero (Indiana Jones) fights off Nazi villains and survives many dangers (snakes, poison, swords, spiders,

Indiana Jones (Harrison Ford) is eye-to-eye with a deadly snake in Raiders of the Lost Ark.

© Lucasfilm Ltd. (LFL) 1981. All rights reserved. COURTESY OF LUCASFILM LTD.

and others) to win a fabulous treasure (the ark) and rescue a beautiful woman at the same time.

Before the U.S. government sends Indy Jones to the Middle East to find the lost ark and discover its magic powers, in the movie we see him in a jungle trying to uncover another treasure. Before he can reach it, he has to escape from several dangers—a giant rock that almost crushes him, some hidden traps, and a tribe of angry natives. After all that—and more—someone else steals the jewels and takes all the credit. Later, that man turns up helping the villains and gives Jones another reason for wanting to be successful in his search for the lost ark.

This action-packed jungle scene is only the beginning of a thrilling movie. Indiana Jones and his friend, Marion Ravenwood, have one narrow escape after another. *Raiders* is like a wonderful version of the old-time serials that people used to see on Saturday afternoons.

Steven remembers those days from when he was young. His neighborhood theater used to show two movies, some cartoons, and one chapter of a serial—a continued story. Every chapter seemed to end with the hero—Tailspin Tommy, Captain Marvel, or Commander Cody—about to be killed, and every one began with an amazing escape from last week's danger. Steven wanted *Raiders* to have the same feeling as those serials.

For example, one of the most exciting parts of the story is a scene in which a truck tries to run over Indy Jones. He grabs onto the front of it and crawls underneath until he is able to climb up the back of the truck. Finally he gets on top of it, slides into one of the windows, and beats up the driver.

The idea for that scene came from a famous movie stunt that was done by Yakima Canutt years ago. Yakima did the same thing, only he crawled between the pounding hooves of a team

© Lucasfilm Ltd. (LFL) 1981. All rights reserved. COURTESY OF LUCASFILM LTD.

Indy Jones in an exciting scene from Raiders of the Lost Ark. *Steven Spielberg wanted this movie to have all the excitement and adventure of the old-time serials he saw as a boy.*

of horses and climbed up the back of a moving stagecoach.

"The film's like popcorn," Steven says of *Raiders*. "It doesn't fill you up. It's easy to digest. And it melts in your mouth. It's the kind of thing you can just go back and chow down over and over again....I love making movies like that."

And when *Raiders* opened, Steven Spielberg and George Lucas flew back to Hawaii and built another sand castle for good luck.

5. Dreams and Nightmares

In the summer of 1982, two movies came out a week apart that both offered the kind of "popcorn pleasure" Steven remembered getting from the movies when he was young. The first, *Poltergeist*, was based on his childhood fears and nightmares. The second, *E.T., The Extra-Terrestrial*, was based on his dreams.

A *poltergeist* is a noisy ghost. That movie begins with a family moving into a new house in the suburbs and finding that the house is haunted. In fact, the little girl in the family is kidnapped by ghosts and then rescued. Everyone escapes safely, but not before a lot of terrifying things have happened to them.

From the MGM release "POLTERGEIST"
© 1982 Metro-Goldwyn-Mayer Film Co. and SLM Entertainment Ltd.

A scary scene from Poltergeist.

The ghosts in the film first come out of the television set. The little girl talks to "the TV people," and they talk back to her. When they first come out to play, she announces, "They're here!"

No wonder Steven calls this picture, "my revenge on TV." He centers the picture on TV because it is such an important part of life in the suburbs. It's like an extra parent, Steven says. And in some ways television is more powerful than a mother and father because it is always fresh and entertaining and does not reach out and tell you what to do.

"In *Poltergeist* I wanted to terrify and I also wanted to amuse," Steven says. "I tried to mix the laughs and screams together." But even though the film is "meant to be a thrill a second, with humor," the people in it are not special in any way. "They're common, everyday types of people to whom nothing really happens until I come along."

Poltergeist also shows something else that Steven thinks is important in his movies. Real life, he says, can be fun to live with instead of "something you run from and protect yourself from" the way he did when he was very young. As a child, Steven was afraid of many things that appear in this movie. He put all those childhood fears into it, including the dark closet where he locked his sisters, and the tree in New Jersey that scared him with its long, twiggy fingers.

Perhaps his willingness to remember the things he was most afraid of is also what gave Steven the courage to make *E.T.* "*Poltergeist* is what I fear, and *E.T.* is what I love," Steven explained. "One is about suburban evil, and the other is about suburban good." Five years earlier, Steven says, "I would have been too embarrassed about what people would think of me to make *E.T.*" And even after he started the movie, he was afraid it was "too soft" for the men in the audience.

If *Poltergeist* is a story based on a scared boy's nightmares and fears, *E.T.* is a miracle movie based on his dreams. It tells what happens to a shy, lonely boy who is badly in need of a friend, and who finds one when a strange little creature falls from the sky and wanders into his backyard. The creature has been abandoned on earth by accident and is lost. He finally gets home again because three children become his friends and hide him from the adult world that seems to be a danger.

The little boy in the story is named Elliot, and it is not an accident that the first and last letters

E.T. reaches out to touch Elliot in a moment of friendship from the movie.

From the Motion picture *E.T.* Courtesy of UNIVERSAL PICTURES.

From the Motion picture *E.T.* Courtesy of UNIVERSAL PICTURES.

Steven Spielberg directs Henry Thomas (Elliot) in E.T.

of his name are *E* and *T*. His role was performed by ten-year-old Henry Thomas. One reason people like the movie is the friendship between Elliot and E.T. The audience really feels Elliot is talking to someone who is alive and not to a machine. When the movie was finished, Henry Thomas said he missed E.T. "He was a person."

The way the two friends meet is typically American. They play catch with a softball. Then Elliot lures the strange creature into the open by laying a trail of candy. Almost half an hour after the movie starts, the audience finally sees E.T.'s face. And it is not a beautiful face.

In fact, it is gray-green in color and looks rather like a turtle. Steven did not want E.T. to be pretty because his real beauty comes from inside—the way he acts and feels about people. And for Elliot, E.T. is a true friend.

Elliot, his big brother Michael, and his little sister Gertie help protect E.T. until he is able to send a message to his spaceship to come back to Earth and pick him up. On the screen, Steven helps keep E.T. a secret from the grown-ups by keeping them out of the picture as long as possible. At first, the adults are only tall, frightening shadows, talking in the night. Then, until near the end of the movie, the audience does not see the

From the Motion picture *E.T.* Courtesy of UNIVERSAL PICTURES.

E.T.'s face is not a beautiful one. Steven wanted his real beauty to come from the inside.

face of any grown-up except Elliot's mother. She is the only one allowed into the children's world.

Steven believes the movie is convincing because E.T. himself was so well designed that he seems real. "It's very important with *E.T.* that everybody who saw the movie believed he could come into their homes to visit," Steven said. But that was not easy to do. In fact, the first version of E.T. did not work at all. Italian painter and sculptor Carlo Rambaldi was asked to help after he finished working on *King Kong.*

Rambaldi made a skeleton out of aluminum and steel. Then he added fiberglass, foam rubber, and plastic to build up many layers of "muscles." Each layer was connected to special controls so that E.T. could make 150 separate motions. With the help of humans—sometimes it took more than ten of them—he could wrinkle his nose or wiggle the four long fingers on each hand.

Actually, there were three E.T.s with mechanical controls, and one that was really a costume for a small person to fit inside. E.T. was only about four feet tall, but his neck could make him grow much longer. That could happen when he was scared, for example. E.T. also talked. In the movie he said ten words, but the voice came from a woman who was 82 years old. Even her voice

From the Motion picture *E.T.* Courtesy of UNIVERSAL PICTURES.

*Carlo Rambaldi stands in front of his sketches
of E.T.*

was changed by electronics to give it a sound that
is not quite human.

In addition to creating E.T., the movie is very
special to Steven for personal reasons. "I put
myself on the line with this film, and it wasn't
easy." But it worked, because "I've allowed myself to be hurt." By feeling loneliness without

hiding from it, and by remembering how he felt when he was Elliot's age, Steven was able to show a world that people can believe in. And the terrible time he had in a high school biology class was turned into a scene where frogs are hopping everywhere. What was painful then, is funny now.

6. *"Movies are My Life"*

"Actually, I don't mind looking the world in the eye, as long as there's a movie camera between us," Steven once said. Now that is changing, and he is beginning to catch up on things that he missed by watching movies so much.

"Movies are my life," says America's most popular and successful filmmaker. "But I can see now that for some people, movies are only a twice a year experience....I wish I could please everyone and make everyone happy. But I can't," he says. "So instead, I've got to think about what makes me happy and secure. I've been too busy to think about that, but believe me, I'm going to start."

Lately, Steven says he has done a lot of thinking about what makes him happy. And he has discovered that "there's a life after movies."

Today, Steven has four large homes, including two in the Los Angeles area. One is a 14-room house in Beverly Hills, not far from the big movie studios. Outside, it's like a jungle, and inside, it might be mistaken for a halfpenny arcade. Throughout the house, there are pool tables, pinball machines, computers, and video games. Steven also likes pets. He has a cocker spaniel that he spoils, and a green parrot that bites him.

One special piece of furniture is his desk. It contains a built-in adding machine, pencil sharpeners, a stereo radio, a color television, a memory telephone, a paper shredder, and even a night light.

Many other things are connected with Steven's filmmaking. In his house, there are framed movie posters on the walls. One room has his collection of movie music—hundreds of recorded sound tracks—which he loves to play.

Steven would rather eat at home than go to a fancy dinner party. When he gets hungry, he often makes a cheese sandwich or a cup of instant soup for himself. At times, he prepares a tasty gourmet meal for dinner after doing his own shopping at a local grocery store.

This is not the way most millionaires act, but Steven isn't like those people who let success go to their head. When he goes to a party, he is often not noticed. "When I go, I'm the guy in the corner eating all the dip," he says.

In fact, apart from his moviemaking, he has a fairly easygoing life. He does enjoy shooting clay pigeons sometimes, and enjoys a regular physical exercise program.

Also, when he is not busy making movies, Steven likes to relax and spend time with his friends. Both in his moviemaking and in his personal life, friends are important to him.

When he was younger, Steven was so busy

with movies that he didn't have time for girls. That has changed, too. In 1986, Steven married actress Amy Irving. Steven's moviemaking projects often took him to faraway parts of the world for months at a time. Amy's acting roles sometimes required her to be away for long periods, too. As time passed, they began to grow apart. After three years of marriage, Steven and Amy were divorced. Though they are no longer married, they remain friends. Steven and Amy had a son, Max, who is now five years old. Steven loves spending time with Max and with the children in his films.

Of all his movies, Steven enjoyed making *E.T.* the most because it was about kids and had 11 children in it. "I'm still a kid," Steven says. "When people call me Mr. Spielberg, in my head I'll yell, 'Don't call me Mister. I'm not a grown-up yet!' "

Children are one reason that Steven is so

From the Motion picture *E.T.* Courtesy of UNIVERSAL PICTURES.

The children in E.T. *were one reason Steven enjoyed making the film so much. Here Elliot rides his bicycle with E.T. hidden in a blanket in front of him and the other kids around him.*

From the Motion picture *E.T.* Courtesy of UNIVERSAL PICTURES.

Steven Spielberg with Drew Barrymore, who played Elliot's sister in E.T.

interested in moviemaking. "I like directing," he says. "Two things make it worthwhile: the fan mail from the kids, and the first sneak preview when strangers see your film."

Because Steven is so involved in filmmaking, he believes it is important to help young people get started in his chosen field. He is proud of all the talented young people he has hired to work on his pictures. "I love giving people their first break," he says, "because I got my break once, and I know how valuable that first time is."

In order to aid students who want to study filmmaking, Steven has worked to update the equipment available at major film schools. He advises anyone who wants to follow in his footsteps: "Go to film school. Any film school."

What does the future hold for the man who has made the most popular movie of all time? Since his great success with *E.T.*, Steven has produced and directed many movies. *Indiana Jones and the Temple of Doom* and *Indiana Jones and the Last Crusade* featured the same hero as *Raiders of the Lost Ark*. *The Color Purple* earned an Academy Award nomination for best picture.

Back to the Future, starring Michael J. Fox, was a big hit with movie fans. *Empire of the Sun*, like *E.T.*, had a young boy as one of its stars. And in *Who Framed Roger Rabbit?*, the star of the show was a cartoon character who acted alongside human actors.

Steven has moved his Amblin Entertainment offices to new quarters at Universal Pictures. He has expanded his production company so that he can personally be in charge of four films each year. He also directs one movie every 18 months.

That schedule is a very demanding one for any person. For Steven, though, it is one that for now has many rewards. While he knows that "there's more to life than movies," moviemaking is still a very important part of his life. And the millions of people who have enjoyed his films hope that he will be able to make many more in the years to come.

The Author

Currently associate editor of *Computer Technology Review*, Tom Collins is an experienced journalist, writer, and editor. He has worked for several metropolitan newspapers, edited for Time-Life Books, and served as the editor of a religious magazine. The author has written books on a wide variety of topics, and he has contributed to a number of reference works, including a major volume on black history and biography.

Mr. Collins has recently completed a critical study of Robert Bloch and the first biography of Carl Solomon. And from his home in Los Angeles, he is ideally situated to keep track of one of his favorite subjects, movies and the people who make them.

92
SPI
    Collins, Tom
        Steven Spielberg, creator
        of E.T.

$14.95   9-93

DATE DUE			

NEW BUFFALO ELEM. SCHOOL LIBRARY